NOW THAT I HAVE YOUR ATTENTION

How YOU can stand out as a speaker or presenter

Colin Williams

Published by Colin Williams and Gannadoo ABook 2021

Copyright © 2021 **Colin Williams**

Colin Williams asserts the moral right to be identified as the creator of this publication.

Illustrations by Kayt Duncan.

All rights reserved. No part of this publication may be reproduced or transmitted by any means or in any form, including electronic, mechanical, photocopying, recording or otherwise, without prior permission from the author.

Information provided is of a general nature only and should not be taken as legal or financial advice. The author, publisher and all agents shall not accept responsibility for damages, loss or inconveniences caused by individuals acting upon advice provided.

A catalogue-in-publication (CiP) record of this book is available from the National Library of Australia.

Book cover design and formatting services by Gannadoo ABook gannadoo.com.au

ISBN:

978-0-6485662-5-0 (pbk)

978-0-6485662-6-7 (ebk)

The purpose of this book is to help you to make, what I call, an R.E.M. transition; to take you from "that's me in the corner" to "that's me in the spotlight".

Colin Williams

Contents

Foreword	vii
Introduction	xi
It's all Greek to me!	15
Pineapple	21
Hurdles, not barriers	29
A tip from Michelangelo	33
The blue note	37
I feel the urge... the urge to purge!	43
But, I'm not funny!	49
Who is this imposter?	53
Get off the "*blandwagon*"	57
There are more people alive today...	63
My favourite teacher	67
Jargon dioxide	71
Check-mate	75
Powerless, POINTless!	79
Like Yoda, speak	85
Having a ball	89
The Nobel Prize goes to...	93
It is OK to make fun of somebody	97

Now that I have **you**r attention

Million dollar story	99
Humility	103
Anatomy of a speech	107
Any questions?	115
Tulips	121
Shut-up and be heard!	125
Nice story. What's the point?	131
Go be spectacular	137

Foreword

Speakers everywhere, this book is for you!

I was thrilled when I heard Colin Williams was planning to share his many lessons learned from years on stage as a public speaker in a book. Having shared a stage with Colin on a number of occasions, and sat in the audience of events he's been headlining, I knew it would be a book rich with wisdom and riddled with tips and ideas that weren't just realistic but adaptable and 100% attainable by anyone prepared to put in the practice.

I share a learning philosophy with Colin; do the work, reap the reward. The reward in this case is unparalleled prowess at communication. Imagine, your message spread far and wide, received, heard, and acted upon. There are plenty of self-help books out there claiming to hold the secrets to becoming a better, stronger, louder speaker before you can even say the word "*speaker*". The faster they claim you can become proficient, the faster you should place it back on the shelf. Colin makes no claim that his account will transform you overnight. On the contrary, he attests straight up that the tips herein are based on his success, and you only

Now that I have **your** attention

take what works for you. As a speaker myself for over fifteen years the only suggestions from peers that have stuck, are those that felt natural and right to me.

Throughout this book Colin generously shares anecdotes, and recalls many positive learning experiences from Toastmasters International® (TMI), a global public speaking organisation that provides thousands of people around the world a forum to practice speaking. TMI's primary goal since its establishment in the 1920's by Ralph Smedley, is to provide individuals with means to improve themselves in business and life. The ability to communicate with confidence and clarity in group situations has been and will continue to be a benchmark for determining success in the western world.

TMI is only one of many communication development organisations. No one organisation is necessarily better than another. When choosing an organisation key considerations include cost, time and accessibility, but most importantly support and camaraderie. Do you feel comfortable? Will you be supported? Do you think you will come back? If yes, then that is the right place for you.

Very few are born with a natural and exceptional oratory talent. The rest of us have to learn it, and constantly work at it. You may be surprised at just how hard some of the greatest speakers you know have worked to fool you into thinking their ability was natural.

I admire Colin's courage to share his ideas and his experiences. He's honest and makes no qualms that not all his advice will be a perfect fit for all readers. Understanding why certain methods work or don't work is always a benefit. Besides, how will you know if you don't give it a go! Don't worry if it doesn't work. Use that experience to build on the next. When something does work, practice it again and again. Each time push yourself just a little further. Aim for that stage with the message you have burning inside you, and don't stop learning.

Now is your time. Take this book, read it, try it, be great. Be that brilliant speaker Colin knows you can be.

Kayt Duncan
Speaker, Entertainer & Publisher

Introduction

It doesn't matter what you think.
It doesn't matter what you know.
It doesn't matter what you dream.
Nothing will come of it...

...if you can't communicate effectively.

Only 8% of those who have a fear of public speaking, seek professional help, despite the documented negative impact this particular fear has on career and wages. This is according to US Public Speaker and founder of MagneticSpeaking, Peter Khoury. He also states the following staggering statistics that the fear of public speaking has been attributed to:

- » 10% impairment of individuals wages
- » 10% impairment of college/university graduations
- » 15% impairment or prevention of promotion to management.

That's quite a toll, simply for being frightened to speak up in group situations and say your piece.

So how many opinions in your workplace have remained unexpressed?

Now that I have **your** attention

How many ideas have remained unspoken?

How many peers have sat silent?

Are you one of them? Or someone you know?

Adept public speakers draw from a range of speaking tools such as strong vocals, body language, eye contact, clear structure and simple delivery formulas. A speaking toolkit comprising these skills and abiding by the rules they espouse will make you a good speaker.

But good is not good enough anymore.

Good is the new average.

If you have a message to deliver, a product to promote, or as they say at TED[1], "*an idea worth spreading*", you must be better than good. You need to take another step up, and be great. You can't just rely on having the courage to speak, you have to speak to be heard, speak to be understood, speak to change minds.

If I have learned one thing in my exploits as a speaker, comedian, writer, musician and filmmaker, it is how crucial connection with my audience is. I have seen too many people

---

[1] TED; Technology, Entertainment, Design, nonpartisan nonprofit devoted to spreading ideas. ted.com

Introduction

squander their opportunity to impart their message because of audience disengagement.

And it's a tragedy.

I have written this book, driven in part, by selfish need. I thrive on witnessing great speeches delivered by great speakers. I am enriched when I sit in an audience and experience idea-challenging presentations. If I can help facilitate a presenter's improvement to become one such speaker who changes and inspires minds, it will be to everyone's benefit, not just my own.

This book will give you some tips and ideas to help you move from good to great, and stand out as a speaker and presenter.

Not every tip may work for you. I suggest you read them, and adopt only those which resonate with your style, and enhance your presentations. If you have to force a change, it's clearly not working for you, Don't worry. It's vital that all speakers remain true to themselves and nurture their own style of communication.

Don't demand my square to be your circle. But do give it a try. Something that looks or sounds like a poor fit, might turn out to be just right!

Now that I have **your** attention

I encourage you to experiment with the ideas in the following pages. Challenge what you already know, or think you know, makes a good speaker or a great speaker.

I also urge you to never settle for *"today's good speech"*, but constantly seek *"tomorrow's great improvement"*.

It's all Greek to me!

The secret to a great speech is not new. Over two thousand years ago the Greek philosopher Aristotle worked it out. He devised the "*three pillars of persuasion*" theory, and it remains as relevant today as it was back then.

Three pillars of persuasion

"*Ethos*" relates to a speaker's character and speech topic qualifications.

"*Logos*" concerns the facts and data reinforcing the speaker's argument.

"*Pathos*" covers a speaker's emotional connection to their audience.

Now that I have **you**r attention

Finding just the right balance between these three elements can be the difference between delivering a good speech and a great speech. Throughout this book, I will refer back to these pillars and their effect on presentations. Let's just have a quick look at each of them now.

Ethos is a tricky part of the balancing act.

As a speaker, you have to provide enough confidence to the audience that you know what you are talking about without coming across as a know-it-all, or braggart. I have sadly seen speakers totally lose engagement with their audience by name-dropping and boasting about their achievements and qualifications. Certainly, these speakers demonstrated aptitude on the subject, but it far outweighed favourable character traits in the eyes of their audience. The result being disengagement due to perceived arrogance.

I don't believe a speech should start with *Ethos*. Acknowledging competence and experience is definitely important early in the first third of any presentation. The priority though is best addressing it with enough sensitivity and thought, that it endorses your character rather than invalidating it.

It's all Greek to me

Logos becomes involved when proving a point.

Differing opinions and arguments need data to support the alternate perspectives. Without supporting evidence a statement is simply empty air and carries no persuasive weight. It is possible and often dynamic to open a speech with *Logos*, especially when the data or fact cannot help but catch attention or shock an audience.

Pathos is about establishing a relationship between you and your audience.

Relationships act as channels of communication. Hostile relationships breed poor channels of communication while relationships of trust are strong and open, allowing the possibility of adaptation, growth, and change on the part of the receiver. This positive connection is precisely what a speaker aims to nurture in an audience.

Pathos is achieved through storytelling, anecdotes, and language devices such as metaphors and analogies. These tools illustrate key points and arguments through common connections in a more mutually open and less direct and definitive manner than Logos. I find the *Pathos Pillar* the most enjoyable part of speaking.

Now that I have **your** attention

A speaker's role isn't just to relay a litany of facts and figures but to find the right balance of all three pillars in order to connect, engage and entertain a crowd. Finding your own balance is key to your audience being as receptive as possible, sharing an open channel of communication and taking your message home afterward to muse on further, or better still to inspire positive change.

Balance can largely depend on the subject matter.

Getting that balance wrong is both a harrowing and illuminating way to understand it. I once started a speech by stating "*I am a genius*". I then backed up the statement by quoting the results of my MENSA[2] entry test. From the moment I spoke my fourth word, I knew I was losing the audience. Their eyes were shifting, there was considerable fidgeting, and the room ambiance deteriorated. The arrogance of someone referring to themselves as a genius!

This is how easy it is to cross the *Ethos* line from credentials to bragging. In four words I

---

[2] MENSA; founded by Roland Berrill and Dr. Lance Ware in England, 1946 as a non-political round-table society for highly intelligent people. https://www.mensa.org/

It's all Greek to me

had insinuated that I was above everyone in that room.

Fortunately, *Pathos* came to my rescue. I wove in a series of anecdotes from times when my decisions and poor choices clearly portrayed me as a bumbling fool. I followed each story with the catch-cry, "*Well done, Mr Genius!*" The shared laughter at my misfortune triggered a mood transformation through the room that was breathtaking. I regained their lost trust by humbling myself and bringing equality back to our channel of communication.

Now with the positive engagement and a receptive audience, I proceeded to discuss how IQ tests work (*Logos*).

In this instance, that particular speech introduction strategy was a risk I purposefully took to test poorly weighted *Ethos* and the recovery power of *Pathos*. The experiment was mortifying, but ultimately a success. Respecting the limits of *Ethos*, nurturing *Pathos* to its full potential and weighing in *Logos* at the optimal point all help balance and maintain the channel of communication. You might have to get it wrong a couple of times to find the balance that works for you. Be prepared for it to continually drift and shift.

Now that I have **your** attention

65:30:5

My rule of thumb for a speech is sixty-five percent *Pathos*, thirty percent *Logos*, five percent *Ethos*. *Pathos* is that important! If you don't make that connection, it is hard to successfully share your message. Whatever balance you use, trust the reception of your audience to let you know if it's right.

Pineapple

Let's define what communication is.

Communication is not exclusively what is said.

It also includes what is heard, understood and acted upon by the recipient. If we speak to an audience, and from that act the audience is not informed, inspired, motivated or entertained, communication has failed.

A speaker's job is to communicate.

A good speaker succeeds at communication.

Now that I have your attention

So, what makes one speaker good but another speaker great? Is it making the odd dynamite speech?

No.

The reputation of "*great*" is endowed on speakers who communicate at a constantly high standard, regularly and consistently. A great speaker achieves more than just the receipt of information by their audience, not once or twice, but every time they communicate.

Consider the difference between the typical handling of a prepared speech and an unprepared speech.

With a prepared speech we have plenty of time to research, write, rewrite, re-research, edit, practice, practice, practice and deliver. Therefore, a speaker presenting with the support of maximised preparation can be confident of maximised success, every time.

An unprepared speech requires thoughts to be gathered in the moment. The resulting communication is unedited and unrehearsed. From my broad and varied speaking experience, I would safely estimate a 50% success rate of unprepared communication.

Pineapple

Great speakers avoid being unprepared, as do great athletes, great actors, great musicians. In fact, anyone who wants to be successful avoids situations of mediocrity and potential poor performance.

Let's insert a bit of *Lagos* here for the statistic lovers.

A speaker presents at 30 separate engagements over a set period of time. Ten of those presentations are prepared speeches and twenty are unprepared. Now apply my estimate of a 50% success rate estimate for all the impromptu speeches. The average of great speeches for our hypothetical speaker is about 67% (trust me, I've experienced the maths!). That success rate is simply too low to meet the criteria of speaking at a constant, and consistent high standard.

The weak area requiring immediate attention is speaking when unprepared.

Or is it?

What if we were to stop making unprepared speeches?

In our theoretical scenario our overall percentage of high calibre presentations would logically hover regularly around one hundred.

Now that I have **your** attention

Unfortunately two thirds or our possible speaking opportunities come from impromptu circumstances. Removing those opportunities from our repertoire would result in a significant loss of speaking practice. Plus, it's nigh impossible to get through life, without being asked to make an unprepared speech?

So consider what I mean by unprepared.

Imagine you are the company accountant asked unexpectedly at a meeting to summarise the current health of the company budget. You should be able to stand up and give a very good account, given it's your job to be on top of that particular information. You might have appreciated more time to hunt for nitty-gritty finessed details, but overall, you have the high-level information that is required at that moment, which is all that is expected. You are prepared. It's your job to be prepared.

If, at this hypothetical meeting, discussion turns to a new project, one you are hearing about for the first time. Suddenly in the spotlight, you're asked to argue the potential impact the project could have on the company's bottom line. This is new data, requiring new facts from new research. In this instance, you are best being

Pineapple

bold enough to defer your reply until you have had time to sift through those nitty-gritty details.

Your deferral is your presentation.

Be prepared to graciously and professionally decline immediate topical response until you can accurately and confidently provide the information being requested. Generally speaking, peers appreciate honesty over fabrication. Your confident ability to acknowledge, in any situation, a need for further time to prepare an accurate response, will result in a successful unprepared presentation. Further, it will lead to an opportunity for a later prepared presentation.

A win-win!

A good rule of thumb is to only talk about that which you know. If it is your job to know something, then know it. That, is being prepared.

An impromptu speech can be a prepared speech, if you know what might be asked of you, or being prepared to say you need more time to gather the required information.

Consider job interviews. Interviewers often ask pre-determined questions from a previously drafted list. It is unlikely that interviewees are ever privy to questions in advance. Interview questions are designed to elicit elaboration of scenario experience. Your experience. Your history. Your knowledge. Information you already have. You can pre-empt what the questions might be and prepare based on those assumptions.

If you go into an interview and are surprised by certain questions, chances are you haven't prepared properly. If there is a question that really comes as unexpected and you can't think of what to say, tell them that. Be honest. Be prepared to decline a comment rather than waffle on for ten minutes about something you have no knowledge about.

I have conducted many job interviews and nothing is more frustrating than the candidate talking for the sake of talking. The harsh truth is, these candidates head straight to the "*no*" pile.

There is an old saying,

> *"Better to remain silent and have everyone think you a fool, than open your mouth and remove all doubt."*

Ralph Smedley, the founder of Toastmasters International said, *"The unprepared speaker has every right to be afraid."*

Pineapple

Toastmasters clubs have a section of their meeting specifically designed to improve off-the-cuff speaking, called *"Table Topics"*. A member is randomly selected to immediately deliver a two-minute speech on an unanticipated topic (*eg. Pineapple*). Many Toastmasters believe this is a good idea, and great for developing cohesive in-the-moment speeches.

I think differently. Questions and answers need purpose.

Note, if you are ever in an interview, and the interviewer says "Pineapple", stand up and walk out. You do not want to work for this organisation!

In the real world, we speak, and speak well, when we have something to say.

Great communicators take as little or as long as necessary to say what needs saying. I do believe any opportunity for club members of a speaking organisation to speak is significant. However, putting them on the spot to speak on a subject of their own choosing would reap more real-world benefits for that individual member.

Hurdles, not barriers

One evening I was attending a Toastmasters club meeting, when a casually-dressed man, in his early thirties, entered the room.

He looked disoriented and anxious, so I approached and engaged him in conversation with the hope of making him feel comfortable enough to stay. He introduced himself as Adrian. It became apparent through our brief introduction this new guest had a developmental disability that was contributing to his social awkwardness. I invited him to sit next to me so I could guide him through the meeting formalities.

Now that I have your attention

The meeting was a constant struggle for him. He fiddled with his phone, emptied and refilled his wallet, and had every appearance of complete disregard for the evening's speakers.

Yet he returned. He attended a second, and a third meeting, and finally formalised membership. Eventually I learned he had Asperger's Syndrome, a form of autism. This was the cause of his social-situation struggles and his difficulty to make eye contact.

He accepted my offer to act as his Toastmaster mentor.

Eventually it came time for him to make his first speech. He spoke of his disability and his plan to speak at a Multicap conference the following year. He battled through that speech and received the customary standing ovation for an inaugural Toastmaster member speech.

He prepared his second speech and emailed it to me. It was well-constructed, articulate, and powerful. It reflected his extensive academic achievements and amplified employment and career prejudices that come with living with a disability. He had prepared a strong speech and I was looking forward to hearing him present it.

Hurdles, not barriers

About one minute into his presentation he moved off script. He started talking about cricket and his hero Shane Warne, and continued in a chaotic and disconnected improvisation through to the end.

> *"What happened?"* I asked when he returned to his seat next to mine. *"Nothing"*, he replied. *"I decided to ad-lib!"*
>
> *"Why? You had a perfectly written script! Let's not do that again. Agreed?"*

With a sheepish grin, he nodded in agreement.

My protege returned to sticking on script, and continued to improve and increase his skills. He successfully orated at the Multicap conference achieving his original goal, and continues to speak regularly at club meetings. His speeches are heartfelt, littered with humour and on point. You wouldn't know listening to him speak today, just how hard he found standing before his first audience, looking them in the eye, and sharing his personal journey.

What is the point of sharing his story?

Public speaking is hard.

No matter how hard you find it, there is likely to be someone who finds it harder still. Take

Now that I have **your** attention

comfort that you aren't alone in feeling that way. Use it. Use the tools that help you control the fear and make the task easier. Stay away from methods like improvisation while you master control and connection. Don't make the task harder than it already is.

Adrian stuck with it. Despite his Autism Spectrum Disability, he absorbed the advice from peers, grew from the experiences that were less than successful, and pulled together his own toolkit full of all the techniques that worked for him.

Our impediments are not barriers, they are hurdles waiting to be leapt.

Whatever those hurdles are, you can become that great speaker if you are prepared to commit wholeheartedly and do the work.

A tip from Michelangelo
(The sculptor, not the ninja turtle)

Michelangelo created the magnificent statue of David from a huge chunk of marble. When asked how he did it, he explained that the statue was always in there. All he had to do was chip away anything that wasn't David.

The same philosophy applies to our speeches and presentations. If we have a thirty-minute presentation to give, I recommend writing ninety minutes of content, from which you cut and chip

Now that I have **your** attention

away at to find the best thirty minutes. Start with more than is necessary and edit it down, taking out everything that is unnecessary.

Anything that isn't our magnificent masterpiece must go.

It isn't easy. Editing can be a painful process, even for the very best speakers. Every minute you spend chiseling away at that metaphorical block is a minute well spent.

There is a technique in speech writing referred to as *"callback"*. This is where you mention something early in the speech and later refer back to it.

While writing a recent competition speech, I mentioned early that, as a child, I loved the TV show Gilligan's Island. Towards the end I wrote,

> *"It doesn't matter if you are a skipper, a first mate, a millionaire, a wife, a movie star, a professor, or a mid-western girl called Mary Anne."*

The line still makes me smile. It's a line that might amuse anyone who loves or even remembers the show like me, but as I chiselled away at my speech I realised the inside joke risked excluding as many audience members as

A tip from Michelangelo

it included, possibly more. Second to that, the wordy list upset the rhythm of the speech at a critical part; the conclusion.

In sculpting terms, it would have been like a large bump on David's nose. It had to go! You could call it literary rhinoplasty.

When I am editing, I am constantly referring to the thesaurus and I don't rest until I find THE word.

In the first draft of the speech mentioned above, I wrote,

> "My father sat beside me and together we watched the fire in silence"

This is a reasonable sentence. But it didn't capture the emotion of the moment I was looking to impress on the audience. Closer chipping sculptured;

> "Dad perched himself beside me and together, without conversation, we admired the ballet of flames, accompanied by the cicada choir."

Now that I have **your** attention

This change gave the moment life on the paper that gave me greater ability to give life to the words on stage.

Mark Twain said, *"The difference between the almost-right word and the right word, is like the difference between a lightning bug and lightning."*

If you don't take the time to refine, to smooth, to polish and finish writing and planning what you intend to say, then you'll never craft the lightning. Your work will never compare to the artists that came before.

Don't be satisfied with a bug. Aspire to perfectly sculpted presentations that are lightning!

The blue note

Western music is usually in major or minor keys. The Blues is played using these scales, but sometimes some notes are flattened, slightly deviating from the strict scale. It adds tension and anticipation.

It is wrong. It doesn't belong. It is outside the rules.

And it sounds great!

Now that I have your attention

These notes are called "*blue notes*".

Folk singer/songwriter Townes van Zante said, "*There are two types of music, the blues and Zippity-do dah.*"

Good speakers learn the rules of speaking and run around delivering good speeches. But, as we discussed earlier, good is no longer good enough. Many of these speeches are Zippity-do dah; the same old thing.

In 1960s London, a young man bought himself a Fender guitar with the intention of being a rock virtuoso. After rubbing shoulders with Jimmy Page, Jeff Beck, Eric Clapton and Jimi Hendrix, he realised that he didn't have the talent to make it as a rock god.

He took his guitar to a second-hand shop to sell it. He walked out of the shop, not with money, but with a shiny, slightly-used flute. Three weeks later he would be the world's greatest rock flautist, virtue of being the world's only rock flautist. The man was Ian Anderson, singer, guitarist and dynamic flute player, with the band Jethro Tull. He became hugely successful producing 22 albums, including number ones in the UK, US and Australia.

The blue note

Finding your "*blue note*" could be as simple as approaching a common message from a different angle than the crowd of other speakers. I can't tell you how many speeches I've heard recently on the topic of mindfulness. It's a solid, broad, and relevant subject to speak on, for so many occasions and audiences. The problem is, there is an abundance of speakers flooding stages, speaking on the subject.

Instead, what if you traded in your message of mindfulness meaning being present in the moment, to mindfulness meaning, treating people kindly by being present in the moment with them? Within three weeks, you could be the world's greatest speaker on "*Kindfulness*" by virtue of being the world's only speaker on "*Kindfulness*".

A great speaker has a "*blue note*". They have played around with flattening and curving messages and deviating from the common theme. Their speeches are distinctive, resonating with their audiences louder, more powerful, and more distinctive than others.

If you recall, I mentioned earlier that **blue notes lie outside the rules**. They were notes that didn't belong. It is for this reason that they work only if they fall naturally into the makeup

Now that I have **you**r attention

of the presentation. They cannot be contrived or overused. If a speaker veers from the rules and it feels laboured or manipulated just for effect, it will simply sound wrong, just as the rules stipulate.

Make no mistake, your content is extremely important, but it must be delivered with your special touch to make it purposeful and truly memorable.

So, how do we find our blue note?

Have a think about yourself. What makes you, you? Is there anything unique or unusual about you, the way you think, your history, your outlook on life, your influences and experiences? It could be a physical characteristic, a striking style, an out of the ordinary hobby or obsession. If you walked into a room full of people what would make you stand out from the crowd?

There is an old saying, "*You can't see the label from inside the jar.*"

Sometimes we are too close to see what is obvious to others, so don't be frightened to ask your friends and family what they think makes you unique and sui generis.

I once took part in a background analysis exercise with a group of speaker friends. We

The blue note

talked in length about our previous experiences to uncover potential rule-breaking blue notes. Many of us had gems hidden in our past just waiting to be pointed out. Gems we had never considered useful or potentially relevant without someone else's external perspective.

One friend had been a magician in earlier years, and had never thought to bring that to his speaking toolkit. One was a gymnast, one a stamp collector, one played guitar, one had written children's books. None of them had used these experiences to enhance their presentations.

They do now!

After that session we all walked away with a different perspective. We had added a new speaking tool to our kit, and the mindset to inject our uniqueness into our presentations. We had found a blue note.

Have another look or listen to your speech.

> Is there a different angle you could look at it from?
>
> Is there another way you can inject yourself into the message?
>
> Are all the notes just right, or is there room to bend or break a rule?

I feel the urge...
the urge to purge!

Imagine you have a fully inflated balloon that you want to blow another breath of air into.

You can't.

It simply won't fit any further air in without the balloon bursting. If you MUST add more air to it, you will first need to release some of the air currently in the balloon, in order to make room for the new breath.

It's not uncommon to hear the random conversations being had by your audience as they enter the speaking venue or while you wait

Now that I have **your** attention

for the event to commence. You can quickly get a sense of the many and varied, and often banal thoughts that occupy their minds.

> *"Did I leave the iron on this morning?"*
> *"What shall we have for dinner tonight?"*
> *"I had an argument with my spouse today"*
> *"I have a report I have to present tomorrow and I'm here, listening to this!"*

These thoughts and many more are whizzing around their minds.

As the presenter, you have information to deposit into their minds. But just like the balloon, their minds are already full of thoughts, and you haven't even started. Before you can pass on any new knowledge or entice any new thinking, you must first make room in your audience's heads by releasing current mind matter and making space for yours.

I call this purging.

The idea of purging is to make your audience forget their present thoughts, push away conflicting immediate concerns, and leave their minds free to absorb your content.

There are many ways to purge an audience.

I feel the urge... the urge to purge!

A few tactics I use that work well include, opening with a powerful statement, showing a graphic slide, or telling a light personable story. Stories work really well. Nothing however, purges an audience like a good laugh. Hitting the audience with humour, particularly at the start of your presentation, clears their minds and generates a connection between you that creates a vacuum for your content, allowing your ideas to fill the void the laughter has left.

I was once asked to deliver an after-dinner speech for a politically active group. I was given twenty minutes to deliver a particular message.

The presentations prior to dinner had been politically heavy, involving debate and some conflict. Dinner allowed for lighter casual conversation but it also scattered the group thoughts away from the central camaraderie theme of the evening. Few people are ready to return to heavy political discourse after a nice warm conversant meal.

I launched with some light comedy, and then spent seventeen minutes telling jokes. I borrowed some from my regular stand-up routine and threw in a couple I had written especially for this engagement. The attendees

Now that I have **your** attention

were rolling in the aisles. At the seventeenth minute, I said, *"If I can be serious for a minute."*

The room fell silent. You could have heard a pin drop. I went into the serious part of my speech. They took in every word, as I encouraged them to continue their good fight. In return I received an enthusiastic standing ovation.

The critical part of the speech containing the message was only three minutes long. However, had I not added that seventeen minutes to let them deflate a little after dinner then it wouldn't have mattered if I spoke for 30 minutes or 30 seconds. The 17 minutes of strategic comedy allowed their dinner and pre-dinner thoughts to vacate their minds so there was room for my message to enter.

I regularly advocate and speak for the Heart Foundation. I talk about diet, exercise and minimising the risk of heart disease. It can be a dry, serious subject. I'll often start my presentation with a powerful fact coupled with humour:

> *"Sixty percent of Australians are overweight or obese".* I am carrying a few extra pounds myself. I point at my body and add, *"Here's one I prepared earlier."*

I feel the urge... the urge to purge!

It never fails to cause a laugh. It's lightened the mood even if the opening statement is *"heavy"* we're off into the presentation on the right foot.

I will never forget the reception I received with the following opening story, which I still rate as one of my more successful purging exercises.

> *When I was young, my family lived in a small house in the bush. We had no power or phone, ran kerosene lights and fridge, cooked on a wood stove, and used an outside toilet, thirty metres from the house, on the edge of the creek.*
>
> *Many times my brother Dave and I begged Dad to install an inside septic toilet, like all the other families on our road.*
>
> *Dad's reply was always, "That toilet is perfectly good. There's no need to replace it while it's in working order."*
>
> *So Dave and I hatched a cunning plan. In the early hours of the morning, we snuck out and pushed the dunny into the creek.*
>
> *The next morning at breakfast, Dad asked, "Who pushed the toilet into the creek?"*
>
> *"Not us Dad"*
>
> *"Let me tell you a story", Dad said. "George Washington cut down his father's cherry tree and his father asked, 'Who cut down the cherry tree?' 'I cannot tell a lie', said George, 'it was I who cut down the cherry tree.' George's father*

Now that I have **your** attention

thanked him and praised him for his honesty. 'Now who pushed the toilet into the creek?'

"It was me and Dave."

He beat the crap out of us.

"But what about George Washington?" *I asked.*

He replied, "George Washington's father wasn't up the tree at the time!"

Ladies and gentlemen, when I said, "he beat the crap out of us" we all laughed. A child being beaten by their father is actually no laughing matter. Domestic violence is about husbands and wives, but it's also about children.

Do you see what I did there?

The contrast between the humour and the serious subject makes it all the more serious. The laughter purged them completely and then the weighty subject hit them like a train. They may not have expected it, but their minds were primed and ready to receive and understand the magnitude of the message.

The power of purging is immense.

The more important the subject, the more vital it is that we plan the opening of our speech with the intention of freeing our audience of unwanted and disruptive outside thoughts, making them as receptive as possible to our new information.

But, I'm not funny!

There are those of you who will say, "*but, I'm not funny!*"

Sure.

It is true that some people are not particularly funny, in their own right. That doesn't matter. What matters is the putting of "*funny*" in, not where it came from.

My wife and I attended a conference at which the keynote speaker started by showing a YouTube video. It was about forty seconds long. It was relevant to the subject. And it was very funny.

Now that I have your attention

After the event, I asked my wife what she thought of the speaker.

"She was so funny", she replied.

"When was she funny?" I asked.

"Her video," she said.

"The 40-second video at the start?"

"Hilarious! She was so funny!"

Hang on a second...

Did I mention the speaker neither featured in the video, wrote the script for the video, or played any part whatsoever in the video, except making it start - at the head of her presentation?

In fact, all the speaker did was, click on an arrow! What's more, my wife was not alone in her reception of the presentation. The speaker was a huge success. Don't tell my wife, but I thought she was funny!

You may be to joke-telling, what Albert Einstein was to basketball. It doesn't matter. If you can understand humour's power to connect you to your audience, and use it as a tool, the same way you use a microphone to project your voice, then *"you are funny"*!

This speaker gave us a great laugh at the start of her presentation. She set herself up for success

But, I'm not funny!

through her careful selection of a relevant humorous tool to lead her presentation.

She purged us.

Humour is the fastest, most universal method to unwind a person, to get them to shed inhibitions, and open a trusted channel of communication between speaker and listener. Those opening 40 seconds of YouTube video was all our speaker needed to relax us.

In the span of the video, she released all the conscious and unconscious blockers filling our minds at that moment. Anything acting as a potential barrier to the mental receipt of her message was eliminated. She had us in the palm of her hands because she used "*funny*".

There is no greater way to entice an audience to be open and accepting of your message, than through shared enjoyment of humour.

There will of course, be occasions when your attempt at humour may fall flat.

I have been asked many times what happens if you say something you think is funny and nobody laughs.

My answer, "*I don't know, it has never happened to me!*"

Now that I have **you**r attention

That's a lie of course! It's happened to me more times than I care to remember and to be honest I don't care to remember.

Just like the internet connection is brilliant one morning and then just won't play ball the next, audiences can be just as unpredictable. Nine times out of ten you might have one line that gets your entire audience belly laughing and then the tenth it falls onto a room of crickets.

My advice is to carry on and forget it. What's past is past. Just as you wouldn't give up if your microphone failed, or your slideshow froze, or the lights flickered. Your next sentence is important and your audience deserves to have it delivered as best you can. The audience came for your message, the humour is just a benefit, albeit a powerful one.

Don't draw attention to it. If the humour didn't work, it didn't work. Move on. By the time you finish your presentation, your audience will have forgotten. You, however, will have clocked up valuable experience swinging a tool that when mastered brings great reward.

So don't worry if you don't think you're funny.

Do "*funny*" anyway.

Who is this imposter?

"Who do you think you are?"

"That's right, I'm talking to you. This is your brain here!"

I have never suffered from this. Oh, unless you count every time I get up to speak! Or draft a speech, or write a book...

Skepticism and uncertainty about ability is disheartening and frustrating, and if not addressed, potentially career damaging.

Imposter Syndrome must be overcome.

Now that I have **your** attention

The qualification to speak to an audience is to know a little more than they do on the topic being discussed. We all have interesting tales to tell, if we look for them, and these stories can articulate any well-presented statistic. Keep in mind that one person's mundane experience might fascinate another. If you stay within the reach of what you do know, and draw from your own experience as evidence your content is qualified.

I recall a time discussing storytelling with my good friend, Roy. He was telling me how unremarkable he felt his life had been. After our conversation had meandered this way and that, we found ourselves chatting about Roy's life as an Indian teacher at an Indian school in South Africa back in the 1980s, when Nelson Mandela was still in jail.

He told me about being tasked with producing a musical event to celebrate International Youth Year.

In Apartheid South Africa, where people lived was determined by their racial group. These areas were classified as "*Indigenous*", "*European*", "*Indian*" and "*Coloured*". They did not mix socially, culturally or educationally.

Who is this imposter?

Roy decided to take on a challenge. He put in a huge effort to convince schools in each of the areas to allow their students to be involved in the cultural song and dance festival called "*Music in Harmony*". He also sought, and received, sponsorship from a local Muslim businessman who shared Roy's vision.

The event was a resounding success.

My jaw dropped listening to his story. Why had I never heard it before? Why wasn't this common knowledge, or in the history books, or first on Google when you search South Africa 1980 Indian culture? This is a story with Bollywood potential. This was certainly not a man who had led an unremarkable life.

Too often we are absorbed by our own ordinary day to day, that we don't see the extra that packages it all up. A helpful prompt can light it up.

The prompt might be that voice declaring you unqualified. We may not all have confronted apartheid, but we have had confrontations, challenges, risks, loss, gains. It's our experiences that make us qualified.

So find your story that illustrates your message and tell yourself to back that self-uncertainty off.

Your story confirms there are no imposters here!

Get off the "blandwagon"

Have you ever watched a television series and thought, "*It's the same story every week, only with different characters or a different setting*"?

Do you feel like you could have written it yourself?

It can happen with speeches too.

Over time many speakers fall prey to the TV serial script drudgery. Formula slips into their preparation. Start with this, follow with that, show a chart here and a picture there. As a consequence, their presentation sounds a lot like the last one.

Now that I have **your** attention

Speech formulas do benefit novice speakers busy building up speaking toolkits. Formulas are a secure and reliable way while you figure out the golden-rules of speaking effectively, and experiment in order to find your personal style.

Speech formulas provide a speaker a less taxing mental investment in the creation of their presentation. The problem is, that many speakers mistake this level of investment as the summit rather than the base-camp. Formulas used for the sole purpose of simplified production run the risk of insipidness.

I call this, *"Getting on the Blandwagon"*.

Good speech writing is a craft. Great speech writing is an art.

Writing a speech needs to be approached with the respect it deserves, acknowledging the substantial weight it carries when determining communication success. If we follow the rules of speech writing and structural formulas too closely, we can end up with something that resembles paint by numbers, an homogenous speech that is the same old banal stuff you hear all the time in the same tedious, unimaginative old style.

Get off the blandwagon

Just as we looked at finding the blue notes to bring jazz to the physical delivery of our presentation, we need to approach the construction of the speech with the same unorthodox challenge.

Just how far can we push the boundaries of structure that the audience expects without confusing the message?

I believe the basic rules of strong, structurally sound content are key. From there you build, push, and test the rules, constantly challenging boundaries, and in the process naturally defy formula generated content.

In one week, I experimented with two different styles of speech construction with contrasting results. The first was a humorous speech written and delivered in the prose and language of William Shakespeare. T'was a resounding success.

The second speech I took the Beatles song titles and crafted them into a careful collage-like narrative. Suffice to say, it was a hard day's night.

If we had to paint a painting, first we would need to learn how to hold a brush. From understanding the mechanism of the brush we move to mixing colours, then creating texture, form, and shade. One lesson builds on another

Now that I have your attention

and each grows in strength and skill because of the lessons that came before and now work with the new lesson at hand.

One foot in front of the other is the only way we can move forward and the only way we can and get our heads around how you paint, long before we even know if we are a Renaissance painter or a manga artist.

Learning the finer techniques of effective speaking employs the same learning principles. Take what you learned from lesson one, two, three, four, etc, and then experiment, at the risk of getting it wrong.

Great speakers push what they know this way and that. They don't churn out yesterday's painting nor do they regurgitate last season's storylines simply because it's easy. Great speakers test for new angles, new themes, new ideas, to bring new "*wow*" to their audience.

Behind all great speakers is a trove of work, and not all of them masterpieces.

How can we take our potentially dull draft and kick it off the Blandwagon? Start with the common rules of speaking.

Push them. Pull them.

Get off the blandwagon

Tug them, tweak them.

Unconstrain yourself, break free, and create your masterpiece!

There are more people alive today...

"There are more people alive today, than have ever died."

Browsing YouTube one day I came across a speech by presentation coach, Conor Neill. His subject was "*How to Start a Speech*". He opined that there are three ways;

» with a question
» a story, or
» what he called a "*factoid*"

Now that I have **your** attention

He used this word "*factoid*", as if it was interchangeable with the word "*fact*". He made the statement I lead this chapter with, as if it was a fact.

If you google "*are there more people alive today than have ever died*", you'll get a list of sites all affirming a similar hypothesis; there are 15 times more people who have died than are currently alive today.

Big deal?

Very. Big. Deal!

If the first thing out of a speaker's mouth is demonstrably wrong, untrue, or a blatant lie, why should we believe anything else they say?

Where is their credibility?

Remember when I spoke about *Ethos* earlier, and reflection of character. Stating falsehoods for fact and standing by it to prove a point, says a lot about one's character. None of it good.

Appropriate research is paramount.

As a speaker, you embody an automatic endorsement of everything you say. If you don't believe something, don't say you do. If you disagree with the message don't persuade others to. Your words reflect your character, so

There are more people alive today

only assert what you know is fact. Leave the factoids for fiction.

One of my favourite TED[3] Talks is by Geoffrey Canada entitled "*Our failing schools. Enough is enough*", quotes astounding student failure rates for American schools over several decades. Geoffrey Canada has spent his life researching and trying to reduce the numbers. Every statistic, every piece of data, is at his fingertips, and he uses them to mount his powerful argument.

There is no exaggeration. No hyperbole. He just delivers the facts with passion. This is integrity. This is ethos.

Let's look at any debate on a current contentious social issue.

What I see far too often, are opposing disputants exaggerating their claims and overstating the risks and dangers of their opposition's case. As a listener, we know both sides can't be speaking the whole or unembellished truth without some elaborate embellishment. This polarisation leads to a distrust of both arguments.

---

[3] Geoffrey Canada: Our failing Schools. Enough is enough! 08 May 2013. Video with sub-titles and transcript; https://www.ted.com/talks/geoffrey_canada_our_failing_schools_enough_is_enough/transcript?language=en

Now that I have **you**r attention

Speakers who speak the plain truth, genuinely earn the audience's trust, and stand out.

Speak passionately on a subject, but don't misquote or inflate data in an attempt to prove your point or disprove your opponent's. Your rectitude will be rewarded with respect from your audience. This is *Ethos*.

My favourite teacher

I want you to stop reading for a minute and think about the best teacher you ever had.

What was her/his name and why were they so great?

Most people will make comments like:

"She was so funny."

"He was so laid-back."

"He made the lessons interesting."

"She involved us."

Now that I have **your** attention

Mr Roberts was my favourite. He taught me English through High School, and he started every lesson with a nerdy joke. The whole class would groan and the lesson would begin. Mr Roberts thought nothing of stopping mid-Shakespeare to tell a topical anecdote, or to ask a member of the class how they thought the scene would play out in modern times. He even got us to recite poetry backward. We never knew what tangent he would be off on next, and we all went along for the ride.

Mr Roberts was *Pathos* personified.

He didn't teach me English. Instead, he instilled in me a passion for the subject, and for that, I will be eternally grateful.

When we recall our favourite teacher, we don't remember what we were taught, we remember how we were taught.

Your audience is no different. To take that step up, as a speaker, we must create an atmosphere that is enjoyable, inspiring and memorable. If we want to be the speaker that audiences recall fondly or profoundly, we must earn the respect and affection of our audience. It might sound a bit egotistical, but we must speak "*with*" them.

My favourite teacher

Imagine a situation where two hypothetical presidents (let's say one is blue and the other is orange) deliver the same speech. Do you think you would appreciate the speech equally, regardless of the speaker or would there be an array of contributing influential factors at play such as regard and respect?

I'm assuming you answered the latter. This is *Ethos* in action. The degree to which the speaker is respected governs the trust the listener places in his/her words.

Jargon dioxide

I once attended a dinner for the Blind Association of Queensland and happened to be seated at the same table as the newly appointed CEO of the organisation who is a sighted man.

In an attempt to start a conversation, I asked him, *"Did you have to learn sign language to get this job?"*

With a smirk, he replied, *"That wouldn't really help with our people."*

I felt so stupid!

Now that I have **your** attention

Using sign language to communicate with people who are blind is a fool's errand. Ineffective. Fruitless. Futile.

Using sign language to communicate with me would be equally pointless and unavailing, as I have never learnt it.

As mentioned in the "*Pineapple*" chapter of this book, communication happens when our message is received AND understood, not with the act of speaking.

It is critically important to use communication that is understood by your particular audience, be that oral or sign, style, language, phrasing, etiquette and formalities, slang or jargon. I've heard my share of speakers littering their presentations with terms and jargon completely foreign to their audience.

I once endured a long session in which an economist spoke to a room of mostly Human Resource (HR) officers, bombarding us all with TLAs. I have had some exposure to the world of finance, but I found myself hopelessly lost, and I wasn't alone. Most of the audience had no idea what was going on. Subsequently, little was learned or gained from that particular presentation. Had the speaker taken into account

Jargon dioxide

the listeners' unfamiliarity with the subject, the presentation need not have been wasted.

By the way, TLA means *"Three Letter Acronyms"*.

See how annoying it is?

It is both exasperating and painful sitting through an hour of acronyms and gobbledygook trying to filter what the actual point is in it all. Eventually you can't help but let your mind wander away to all the other pressing things filling your mind, and tune out of the presentation altogether.

I don't recall where I heard it, but I remember hearing this called, *"Jargon Dioxide"*. It can poison the presentation.

Acronyms and jargon need to be handled with care, just like your audience.

Make no assumptions on behalf of your audience. Treat all information as though it is a potential hazardous subject to your audience. Do your research and ask questions up-front so as to determine what qualifications your audience has so you can be confident your choice of words will be understood.

If you ever aren't sure, take a moment to clarify what your acronyms mean, just as you

Now that I have **you**r attention

would run through the warnings of entering a hazardous area.

Get your language right before you start. Be confident that you and your audience understand each other. Your goal is to communicate, not annihilate.

Check-mate

My father was a pretty decent chess player. Certainly he was more skillful than I have turned out to be. Whenever we played, he gave me an advantage by playing without his queen.

The queen is the most powerful, versatile piece on the chess board. As a result of the impediment he imposed on himself, he became impressively proficient using his bishops, rooks, knights and pawns. When playing other comparable opponents he adopted a similar strategy, sacrificing his queen through the destruction of theirs.

Now that I have **your** attention

With the strongest pieces on the board removed, my father often found himself in an advantageous position of strength, as his adversary did not have his practiced queen-less play.

All speakers could do with a strategic advantage. Imagine the potential of our on-stage success if we could capitalise on every tool inside our speaking toolkit, using each and every asset to its optimal capacity.

Here's a challenge for you. Think about your body-language, and how you currently physically express yourself and utilise the space on your stage. What part of your body do you use really well? Is it your hand gestures? Maybe it's stage movement, or facial expressions.

Now shut them down. Practice presenting without that physical tool.

For example, if you use movement across the stage well, practice with your feet in a cardboard box.

If your forte is hand movements, practice with your hands behind your back. If you have dynamite facial expressions, wear a blank, featureless mask.

By crippling your armoury of your dominant asset, you will naturally enable development

Check-mate

and increase proficiency of your other body language tools, improving your overall arsenal.

I have always had a natural ability to move confidently and effectively about a stage. I find purposeful movement helps bring my stories to life. Enter COVID-19!

Stage movement is seriously restricted when delivering online.

I had been looking forward to competing in the annual Toastmasters Humorous Speech contest on a grand stage before a large live audience. The year's social gathering restrictions had other plans and the speaking contest was held via Zoom.

This meant my physical dynamism would be significantly compromised, contained inside 1080 pixels.

Fortunately, I had deliberately worked at strengthening the other aspects of my body language (hand gestures, facial expressions) and I was able to compensate for my loss of mobility and master this unfamiliar medium and its spatial confinement. I finished second at the highest level.

Check-mate!

Powerless, POINTless!

"He's going to do a presentation. I hope he has lots of PowerPoint slides with loads of dot points and graphs, and I really hope he reads every word on the screen", said nobody ever!!!

Everybody remembers Martin Luther King's famous speech. We all recall so well when he said, *"I have a dream"*, clicked his infer-red pointer and a picture of a dream bubble wiped left to right on the screen behind him.

No, he didn't!

Now that I have your attention

Think back on every great or notable speech in history. How many are memorable because of their supplementary visual or audible extras?

Any?

The speeches that pop into my mind were historic and memorable for the words and the power and passion with which they were spoken.

I have seen few PowerPoint presentations that truly enhance or magnify the weight of the spoken words. And I've seen a few! Poorly designed, and poorly operated PowerPoint presentations have the potential to counteract a powerful performance and impede a presenters message.

That is why I refer to them as *"Powerless POINTless"*.

In 1987, two gentlemen called Gaskins and Austin, invented some software called *"Presenter"*. After a shaky beginning, the product evolved into PowerPoint in the early 1990s, and has since established itself in business as a prevailing presentation tool, adopted by an insurmountable number of employees.

So why would PowerPoint encourage more people to present?

Powerless, POINTless

I think it could be that people who have an aversion to public speaking find PowerPoint presents as a shield between them and their audience. The screen draws the audience's attention away from the speaker, removing them as the primary focal point, and subsequently creating a sense of safety for them from the undesirable task.

So, we end up with a multitude of mediocre speakers presenting subpar speeches propped up by visuals in the belief that fancy slides hide uninspired content and/or presenters. A bit harsh?

PowerPoint is a tool. When used expertly, it can be a powerful tool. Unfortunately, it is too often used incorrectly, inexpertly!

Without the right care and attention, slides can have the opposite effect to what the audience expects. Visuals that don't align or tightly sync with the words being spoken, distract the audience and obscure the message.

The words of a speech only account for part delivery of the message, and successful communication. Body language and voice variation are critical companions. These components of successful communication require direct audience attention

Now that I have **your** attention

to the speaker, not a screen filled with text or dancing gimmicky images.

We are the presentation. We are the speech. We must be the centre of attention.

I recommend writing out your presentation as a complete, or as close to complete, speech as you can. Then ask yourself, which parts absolutely need a slide to harness the point or assist audience clarity. If there are no points that truly need visual clarification, then no PowerPoint accompaniment is required.

Leave it out. I dare you!

PowerPoint should only be used if there is no other way to relay specific information.

There are many alternate visual aids. When inspirational speaker, Simon Sinek, delivered his "*Finding the Why*" speech[4], he used a flip chart. It seemed so organic, so personal.

---

[4] Simon Sinek, How great leaders inspire action TED talk 11 March 2014; https://www.ted.com/talks/simon_sinek_how_great_leaders_inspire_action?language=en

Powerless, POINTless

Props are great visual aids, and have been adopted time and again in powerful presentations. Steve Jobs used a real iPhone. Bill Gates had a jar of mosquitos. Jamie Oliver had a wheelbarrow.

Visual aids can certainly enhance your presentation, if used correctly.

But, practice!

Just as easily as they can aid a speech, they can ruin it by disengaging your audience.

Think twice. Choose wisely. Practice.

Like Yoda, speak

I have a particular speech that begins with the following words:

> "You are, without doubt, the biggest bunch of no-hopers I have ever had the misfortune to stand before."
>
> (PAUSE)
>
> Ladies and Gentlemen,
>
> (PAUSE)
>
> "These were the words of my Year 9 French teacher, the day she gave back our test results."

Now that I have **your** attention

I could have opened this speech with,

> "My grade nine French teacher once said, "You are……. etc.",

but the impact I was after would have been lost.

The order in which words are spoked should be carefully considered to evoke and maintain the interest of the listener.

How many times have you heard;

> "On Monday we were in Paris.
> On Tuesday we were in Berlin.
> On Wednesday we were in Amsterdam."

Do you agree the following is more interesting to the ear?

> "Monday found us in Paris.
> Berlin was our destination on Tuesday.
> We landed, on Wednesday, in Amsterdam.
> Thursday, we decided we needed a better travel agent!"

Too often speakers become monotonous and uninteresting simply because they don't vary their sentence structure or play around with words and synonyms.

Like Yoda, speak

I have found an effective and winning way to practice changing the shape of sentences. I try to create rhyming poetry. When it is impossible to rhyme the last words of certain lines, I'm forced to rearrange the sentence to put the right word in the right place to establish the rhyme. This gets me in the habit of reconstructing sentences to add variety and energy. Regardless of whether the speech is delivered in verse.

> *Where you sit now,*
> *I sat then*
> *Where you have a keyboard,*
> *I had a pen*
> *Poetry, what a bore*
> *Simile, metaphor*
> *Onomato-bloody-poeia*
> *Such words filled my heart with fear*
> *But no*
> *You see, the English language is the ear of a sow*
> *It was back then, it still is now*
> *But through the magic we call verse*
> *We can create a silken purse*

Our sentences should be played with, manipulated and stretched. It's not always easy, and does add preparation time, but effort tends to equal reward. Plus, it's interesting. It's attention-grabbing.

Now that I have **you**r attention

Remember that "*blandwagon*" I spoke about earlier?

If you get in the practice of constantly adapting how your words fall down onto the page, your delivery is unlikely to be considered predictable.

Adding complications to word-smithing forces greater thought resulting in easier listening.

It's also a lot of fun!

Having a ball

How can we expect an audience to become passionate about our subject, if we deliver it in an indifferent, apathetic manner?

Every year, my wife and I travel a couple of hours south to attend Bluesfest at Byron Bay in New South Wales. Five days of live music covering many genres. We see some of the big names from the past, some of whom may be past their use-by date now, and we discover many lesser-known artists and bands, soon to become favourites.

Now that I have **your** attention

I have noticed over the years, key elements I use to rate these entertainers. I enjoy seeing those who are technically adept in their musicianship. I revel in hearing clever lyrics and catchy tunes. But the most important factor in determining my enjoyment, is the amount of fun the performers are having.

There is nothing I enjoy more than seeing a band, laughing together, playing off each other and thoroughly having a ball.

When the performers emit enthusiasm and energy from the stage, I can't help but absorb their passion and love for what they are doing. I can't help but be filled with joy in return. Passion is contagious, and an audience is inevitably swept up in the euphoria.

Two years ago my wife dragged me to see Tom Jones. I was less than thrilled at the invitation and went with low expectations. More fool me!

The seventy-eight year old had surrounded himself with a dynamic eight piece band and they rocked! I'm not ashamed to say it!

Sir Tom harnessed the energy of his young ensemble, laughing, sweating and high-fiving through an hour of pure musical ecstasy. I wondered what Tom would say if I asked him if

Having a ball

all his shows created so much energy. He would probably reply, *"It's not unusual"*.

This is how we should make our audience feel. We should show our passion for the subject by enjoying speaking about it and having fun. In fact, aspire to enjoy yourself. Ooze passion, have a ball and become contagious.

The Nobel Prize goes to...

So, you have a speech to deliver on

> "*New ordering methods for stationery*", or
> "*My work trip to Darwin*", or
> "*How to make pasta*".

Fairly boring, bland subjects, that offer little inspiration to you as the speaker. How much effort should we squander on speeches like these?

Let's jump forward in time. It's five years later and you have devised a plan to end world hunger. You have a critical opportunity to present your

Now that I have **your** attention

findings and convince backers to invest in your globally relevant idea.

Remember those boring speeches you thought too insignificant to invest in? It's now those speeches, and the choice you made in the past whether to harness their merit, that will determine your success now.

Why? Because every opportunity to speak is an opportunity to practice at preparing and presenting sensational pitches that will have everyone captivated. Every time you speak helps prepare you for the speech that just might earn you a standing ovation, a flood of investment and a Nobel Prize. Maybe not today, maybe not in five years. But then again, maybe.

At one of my Toastmasters clubs, we occasionally have an evening called "*Surprisingly Awesome*".

The evening's speakers are all given a week to research and deliver a speech on a group-agreed "*boring*" topic.

One evening I was required to speak about "*shipping containers*".

Ho-hum. I could have gathered data on the history of shipping containers, their dimensions, or maybe just how many are on the water at any given time. During my research I discovered

The Nobel Prize goes to...

the staggering number of containers that fall overboard each year and the very real nautical hazard these accidents cause particularly to smaller boats.

My presentation angle became: *"Man-made icebergs!"* I delivered the speech through the eyes of a yacht captain with a message to be safe at sea. It was titanic!

Every opportunity we have to speak is an opportunity to hone our presentation skills. If we put our heart and soul into every speech we make, no matter how bland the subject, it will put us in a marvellous position when we eventually have something important to convey or urgency to persuade.

I never miss an opportunity to speak. When I was just branching into public speaking, I once travelled over three hours to speak for a mere twenty minutes, because it was a new opportunity to address a large audience and practice something new.

If someone asks you if you're interested in speaking at an event, be it large or small, say "Yes". If you are asked to talk about something that sounds dull at first, say "Yes".

Now that I have **you**r attention

Do the research, find the facts and take control of the narrative.

You never know where your next speech might lead.

Maybe to Oslo to pick up your prize.

It is OK to make fun of somebody

It is OK to make fun of somebody.

It is OK to put somebody down.

There is, however, one proviso. One unbreakable golden rule. One bold and underlined clause in the contract!

That somebody must be you!

Self-deprecating humour is a wonderful tool. It lets the audience know that you are not coming from a place of arrogance or smugness.

Now that I have **your** attention

I was once demonstrating a point in front of an audience of about fifty. I was using a turkey baster to transfer blue-dyed water from one container to another. There was a blockage in the end that caused the device to split in two, covering me in navy-blue water. After a couple of seconds of shock, I laughed and continued the presentation resembling a smurf.

The comical unexpected mishap turned out to be something I could refer back to, throughout the remainder of the presentation when I wanted to give the audience a laugh.

You need to be careful not to push self-deprecation so far that it encroaches on your professional reputation.

The one thing never to self-disparage, is your appropriateness as a speaker on the subject you are presenting.

The audience can laugh at our personal weaknesses and tribulations, but they must never be left in doubt that our expertise in our field will add value during the session.

Million dollar story

Imagine a million dollars. On a table. In front of you.

I once delivered a presentation skills workshop to a group of not-for-profit managers. I opened the program with a hypothetical activity, in a similar vein, for the group:

> "Let's imagine that I am going to give one of you this million dollars, to donate to a charity of your choice, that is not the charity you represent today.

Now that I have **your** attention

I want each of you to tell everyone the name of your selected charity and what they do. When everyone has spoken, I will decide who gets the million dollar charity benefit."

Each of the participants came up and delivered the information as instructed.

One attendee nominated the Cancer Council for their work in research. Another picked the Fred Hollows Foundation for their work on eye health in underprivileged countries. Lastly a quiet participant, Jeff, said he wanted to donate the money to The Smith Family because they provided breakfasts for underprivileged children at schools.

When the exercise was complete, I told them I had decided to delay my decision till the following day. I wanted them to use the night to improve their nomination. I asked them to choose a relevant personal story, that embodied the work of the charity they endorsed.

They would couple this story with the same information they had just presented; the charity name, and what they did that deserved the money. The story didn't have to be a personal experience, but did have to come from someone

Million dollar story

they knew. They had to somehow be emotionally connected.

What an impassioned morning!

Jeff's story was particularly poignant. He shared a personal childhood memory I recall vividly:

> "When I was eight years old, I used to climb the drainpipe of our house, so I could sneak through my mother's bedroom window and steal coins from her purse.
>
> The shame of stealing from my own mother!
>
> But I needed those few cents to buy something to eat at school. My mum would never wake up until around lunchtime because of the booze and drugs. There was never food in the fridge, and hunger pains were the only constant in my life.
>
> No child should have to go to school hungry. I want to give the money to The Smith Family who provide breakfast for thousands of Australian kids."

There wasn't a dry eye in the room. I'm only sorry that my million dollars was imaginary.

How much more powerful was the hypothetical appeal once the story was included?

Every person who presented that day, had a story to tell. Every story had a way of grabbing the audience's heart strings. The stories were true, personal and sentimental.

Now that I have your attention

They weren't complicated.

Yet still brought a depth and connection between speaker and audience that simply did not exist the previous day with the first run of the activity.

> Stories are priceless!
>
> Stories are *Pathos*!

You need that million dollar story in your speech.

Humility

When a speaker presents in front of an audience to inform, influence, or inspire, they must be very careful not to appear as a smug know-all.

I once spoke at a Royal Geographical Society event alongside two other key presenters. The former was a professor who headed a team that had researched and archived historical survey maps. Although he mentioned the team of six in his introduction, he clearly favoured the pronoun "I" throughout the remainder of his speech. His grandstanding bluster was not lost on the audience.

Now that I have your attention

The latter speaker was an amateur photographer who showed a series of photographs of the Mary River. He apologised for the quality of some pictures, and acknowledged the generosity of the club-mate who crewed and drove the boat during the project.

The contrast of the two performances was stunning.

After the formalities were completed, attendees were invited to mingle with each other and the event's speakers. The photographer was swamped with comments and questions from inquisitive and interested people, whereas the professor sat in the corner with the president of the society, devoid of audience enquiries.

Of the two, the professor arguably offered the more impressive scientific contribution to the event, however the photographer sparked significantly more interest by virtue of modesty and recognition of others.

The tone and attitude adopted by a speaker is paramount to positive audience engagement. A speaker's role is not to impose, but to share and encourage thought and consideration of a message. Modesty and humility, as well as servitude, are critical connection points to

Humility

audience engagement. Without that connection to the audience, there is little chance of speech message being received, or at the very least remembered.

Be humble and vulnerable.

Be accessible, and be heard.

Anatomy of a speech

On the following page is a speech I delivered early in my Toastmasters journey. I'll let you read it and then I will discuss some of the elements I used to make this a speech that stands out. It was my first contest.

Now that I have **you**r attention

TITLE: **Forbidden Love**

In this place, it is considered forbidden love.
In this place, it is love, I dare not
speak its name.

Ladies and Gentlemen,

Sometimes one's love is so intense, that one feels compelled to shout it from the rooftops. Such is my love.

So, tonight, with you as my witnesses, I wish to declare my love for...

the word Um.

Um, Um, sweet Um. Though this speech may cost me a fortune in fines, I will not deny you.

When I am without words, I am with words because of you.

When my vocabulary deserts me, it is you, sweet Um, who comforts me until it's inevitable return.

There are those who mock you and deride you. For goodness sake there is usually someone in this room whose sole purpose it is to punish, through humiliation and financial means, anyone who dares associate with you. And I take "Um"brage at that.

We have been together for "Um"pteen years, and in all that time, you have been ever-present, ever vigilant, ever reliable. And I thank you for that from the bottom of my heart.

But my message tonight is bitter-sweet. Although I am declaring my love for you, I

Anatomy of a speech

am also informing you that we must part. You see, I have had to choose between you and my future as a public speaker. The two cannot coexist. They are mutually exclusive, and I have chosen the latter.

What's brought this about?

I have been listening to some of the greatest speakers of all time, delivering some of the greatest speeches of all time, and I've learned that they all have one thing in common.

Your absence!

I wondered if these speeches would have been as effective had you been present.

Had Winston Churchill said "We will fight them on the UM beaches", would he have inspired his nation to such a degree?

Had Emmeline Pankhurst said "Give us freedom or give us UM death", would women have had to wait a little longer to vote?

Had Martin Luther King Junior said "I have a UM dream", would we have seen a black man in the White House?

I've realised that your easy nature has a poison that destroys any prospect of great communication. So I have decided to end our relationship.

It's not the end of the world. It's not as though you'll be lonely. There are many, many, many speakers who will still associate with you. Some in high places. I understand some of our politicians are quite fond of you.

You may well ask, will I replace you with another?

Now that I have **your** attention

The answer is No.

There will be no errs or ahs for me. When I replace you, I will replace you with nothing, with silence, with the eloquent dramatic...pause.

Now, I realise you will still linger in the ether, like a siren sweetly singing, like a temptress trying to seduce me. I know my flesh is weak and, on occasions, I may succumb to your seductive charms. But as the days, and months, and years go by, our rendezvous will become fewer and fewer, until in time, we will be but passing acquaintances.

We've had a good run, but now it's time for me to cut the "UM"bilical cord and set myself free.

Sweet Um, I've loved you oh so much.

You've been my friend, my aid, my crutch.

But now my dear, the time has come,

To say farewell my sweet, sweet Um.

Now let me run through some of the devices I used to make this speech different.

The audience were Toastmasters, so I picked a relatable subject to them.

Many Toastmasters clubs generally nominate a member at meetings to count "*Ums*", and other verbal crutches, said during a speech. Some clubs go so far as to fine members for using "*filler*" words in an attempt to curb the habit.

Anatomy of a speech

My satirical approach to the subject was a guaranteed winner.

Let's look at the title. At Toastmasters, you are introduced by your name and the speech title. That's a little different to corporate presentations, but the need for supplying a dynamic introduction follows similar logic.

When people ask me about this particular speech today, they refer to it as "*the UM speech*". If I had titled it that, I would have lost all the suspense and intrigue I wanted to open with. The opening twist and punchline in my ending would be blown. The title "*Forbidden Love*" gives them no clue to the actual contents other than eliciting cheeky playful thoughts.

The introduction and the words it comprised were delivered in a serious manner.

> *"In this place, it is considered forbidden love.*
> *In this place it is a love we dare not speak*
> *its name."*

It sounds like I am about to speak on a taboo subject. I purposely tried to make the audience squirm with nervousness. When I reveal the word UM as the focus, all the tension breaks and the laughs explode.

Now that I have **your** attention

Unusually, I address an imaginary character throughout the speech, instead of the audience. I have never seen this done and it is the only time I have used this style. It is risky because eye contact is a strong link to your audience, so speaking to a figment requires an intensity that draws the audience's focus with it.

The language isn't casual. I wrote it in a formal style, as if it were a letter to a jilted lover.

When I first started writing a speech about the verbal crutch, I wanted to challenge myself to approach the topic from the opposite direction most Toastmaster colleagues would take. I wanted to see a world where UM was good. It was only after playing around with the concept, that I struck the idea of ending my relationship with UM. Through humour I knew this angle had potential for a strong message for the intended audience.

I stumbled upon the idea to use the UM words, "*umbrage*" and "*umpteen*", for laughs and hunted for any words beginning with UM. There needed to be a balance. Too many uses, risked the speech becoming contrived and tacky, too few and the word-smithing would be lost. I used two "*Um*" words early in the speech to create

Anatomy of a speech

an expectation and tease. I neatly closed the suspense when I said "*umbilical*" near the end.

You will notice that I used groups of threes on a few occasions,

- » ever present, ever vigilant, ever reliable,
- » Churchill, Pankhurst, King.

This is referred to as the "*rule of three*".

Groups of three are said to be effective in speech-making. There are four reasons for this (joke).

I use it but I don't overdo it as it sometimes can appear artificial.

All these elements:

- » careful planning of the speech introduction
- » dynamic conscientious consideration of opening lines to maximise audience engagement
- » playful and experimental use of stage and physical presence, in this instance through an imaginary character
- » precise and meaningful attention to scripting and word use
- » specific scrutiny and care for repetition and other audience attention devices

Now that I have your attention

combined to create a speech that was a little different from a typical run-of-the-mill take on a common subject. It worked, I won.

Novelty is captivating.

Look for small ways to make your presentations stand apart from the crowd.

Any questions?

Personally, I love a good Question and Answer (Q&A) session.

The time allocated to accommodate questions from the audience in your presentation accomplishes a couple of things; clarity and revision for the audience, and a window of potential improvement for you and your presentation.

The Q&A part of a talk provides audiences the opportunity to clarify and reconfirm specific points raised throughout the presentation. Engaged audiences jump at the chance to obtain

Now that I have your attention

finer detail or receive extended, elaborated explanations that might have been necessarily abbreviated in consideration of time. ,

More importantly though, the Q&A session is an opportunity for a speaker to identify weaker parts of their presentation that consistently draw questions concerning clarification. Similarly, Q&A's can highlight areas that would benefit from an update or edit. Great speakers continually collate queries and discussions generated from Q&A's and hold them in trust as potential material for future talks.

I have, however, seen some Q&A's go terribly wrong. Tragically wrong.

On these occasions I understand why many speakers shudder at the thought of handing the floor over to questions. In today's market though, most speakers will be expected to include time for audience questions. So let's do it right.

There's always a risk that question time will leave your presentation flat, particularly if there are no questions. For this reason, try to avoid leaving your Q&A right at the very end. Instead, strategically place it before your conclusion. This way you have the freedom to incorporate any

Any questions?

fresh ideas that emerge from your responses, or from a naturally evolved conversation with the audience, into your well-rehearsed, dynamic and memorable conclusion.

More importantly though, by saving your conclusion till AFTER your Q&A you can quickly re-engage and recover from an awkward or apathetic audience by smoothly transitioning out of the Q&A into your presentation wrap-up seamlessly. Thus saving yourself, and your audience, from an uncomfortable and inelegant ending to an otherwise great session. .

While we're on the subject of questions, remove the statement "*Good question*" from your repertoire!

Avoid the "good question" auto-reply like the plague! Please!

It devalues any question that has not received this comment previously or will receive in the future. Some speakers have a tendency to say "good question" after every question, as an unconscious way of affording themselves thinking time.

A stronger strategy is silence. If you need to think for a moment to clearly and coherently answer a question, then do just that. Think.

Now that I have **your** attention

You don't need your mouth to think.

Audiences appreciate answers born from thought. They don't appreciate thoughtless answers. In return for your silent consideration to frame a reply, audiences allow surprisingly respectable amounts of time.

The late Sir Ken Robinson, well known for his many powerful creativity and education speeches, told the story about the time he hosted a panel discussion at a conference that boasted, among many of it's keynote presenters, the Dali Lama. During the panel the Dali Lama was asked a deeply intricate question. Before replying, he was silent for over a minute. The audience waited patiently in anticipation of a profound answer. When he finally spoke, he said *"I don't know."*

How refreshingly honest.

If the Dali Lama can acknowledge, after thinking long and hard, that a satisfactory answer is beyond his reach, then so can the rest of us. Earlier in my chapter about credibility I stressed the need for truth at all cost.

We earn the audience's respect when we answer truthfully.

Any questions?

Respect from your audience is so easily lost if we fabricate replies. There is nothing wrong with the answer *"I'll come back with that information after further investigation"*.

Tulips

If, in a field of lawn, a tulip blooms, that tulip will stand out.

If, in that field, many tulips bloom, then the field will stand out.

The same principle applies to business. If an organisation has one great communicator, that individual will stand out. If that organisation has many great communicators, the organisation will stand out.

Now that I have **you**r attention

If you are an entrepreneur, business owner, CEO, or manager, it is quite possible that you are the standout communicator in your business. Typically, promotion to these higher management positions, requires above average communication skills.

Regardless of whether you are, or aspire to, senior management, I put this question to you: what is more important; that you stand out in your organisation, or that your organisation stands out in it's field?

Imagine every key member of your staff are exceptional communicators. Imagine enjoying effective, clear, dynamic communication with your customers, your suppliers, and dynamic open communication between staff and departments within your organisation.

Your organisation would hold tremendous competitive and economic advantage and prosperity in addition to attracting and retaining passionate, engaged staff.

It doesn't have to be a dream, but it does have to be worked at.

Effective communication is not innate. It must be learned and practiced like any skill. Business promotions often push people into positions

Tulips

with public speaking responsibilities based on unsubstantiated assumptions that because they are experienced at their job they have the tools to effectively speak in public. This is crazy!

For tulips to bloom, the conditions must be favourable; full sunlight, ample nutrients and water. Similarly, staff require conditions conducive to lush environmental growth to bloom. It's not just enough to have a team of highly educated, informed and well experienced people.

The field of green leaves only becomes impressive when the flowers bloom, and for people, that requires the combination of industry-knowledge, and an ability to communicate and share that knowledge, to train and collaborate with other tulips around them. It is the combination that greatly enhances an individual's personal value and, in turn, the value of the organisation.

I encourage you to check-in on your environment.

- » Are you in a place of growth?
- » Are those around you?
- » Can you elicit change through specialised public speaking training?

Invest in communication, fertilise through training, and create that outstanding field.

Shut-up and be heard!

"If you make listening and observation your occupation, you will gain much more than you can by talk."

Robert Baden-Powel.

It might seem counterintuitive to be speaking to communicators about saying nothing, but I believe silence is one of the most valuable weapons in our communication armoury.

Hear me out!

Now that I have **your** attention

Listening can contribute to all three pillars of persuasion.

> » Listening creates *Pathos* because an audience feels involved when their opinions are sought, heard and addressed.
> » There is no better way of gathering *Logos*, than listening to the facts and figures supplied by the organisation or industry to whom you are presenting.
> » *Ethos* is established with all stakeholders through the professional approach to wholly understanding all relevant nuances before attempting to speak on them.

So often, when a problem is presented, there is a clamour to find the solution.

And problems present themselves constantly. So much noise!

I prefer to sit back, silent, and listen to the different contributions, arguments and solutions on offer from others. Only when I have had time for all the incoming information to sink in, will I offer my suggestions. Unless I'm directly asked, I hesitate to add to the racket unnecessarily.

This makes the task of hearing deserving opinions far easier.

Shut-up and be heard!

Resolution comes from the best idea, not the first idea or loudest idea. We only know what the best idea is when we've had time to sit back, hear everything, and think, analyse and weigh all contributions against each other.

If an idea comes forward, from amongst the fray, that I concur is best, then when it becomes my turn to speak I will endorse it and acknowledge the person who made the original suggestion. Even had I determined a matching conclusion prior to hearing another's contribution, I would redirect acknowledgement and praise to the other contributing party.

Praise where praise belongs does a couple of things. It shows you are a team player. Strong teams aren't built from individuals hungry for self-credit. Strong teams exist when peers hold each other up. A gift of praise also makes a deposit in your *"emotional bank account"* with the other person.

An emotional bank account is an idea espoused by Steven Covey, author of *"The 7 habits of highly effective people"*[5]. The account represents your relationship with other people. If you do

---

[5] "The 7 habits of highly effective people" by Steven Covey, first published 15 August 1989; ISBN 9781760856823, 496 pp

Now that I have your attention

the right thing by someone, you are making a deposit into the emotional bank account you have with them. A withdrawal is made when you do something that upsets them.

The idea is, that if you have made sufficient deposits prior to a withdrawal, you can still be in credit and maintain a positive relationship. This is not to be done cynically.

Helping others shine is a great way to foster team spirit. It works particularly well when praising someone who considers themself your nemesis. Sportively, it messes with their head. "*Did he just say my idea was genius?*" But more importantly, positively addressing friction prone relationships helps build strong, sustainable bridges between the weaker parties.

No team can reach its full potential when factionalised.

Of course, this praise must always be warranted, otherwise it risks coming off as sarcasm. If you have stopped talking and been listening, you will know when, and where, endorsement can be productively directed.

The most important time to sit back and be quiet is when you are the most senior person at the table.

Shut-up and be heard!

If you offer up a suggestion first, you run the risk of "*Emperor's new clothes*" syndrome, where people fall into line behind the boss, with little opposition or contribution. A good boss wants to harvest the ideas of their people.

Remaining silent broadens the conversation and allows others to emerge from the shadows and shine. These are the times when we learn individual strengths and identify future leaders. If you aren't the most senior person at the table, are these the characteristics you'd like to see in whoever is?

When you become the person who sits back and listens, speaking only when there is something important to say, or all other ideas have been put forward and you alone can weigh in on the gamut, you will gain a reputation for your wisdom.

When you do start to speak, your audience will think, "*They're about to speak. This will be worth hearing*", and will shut up and listen.

That is a powerful position to be in.

That kind of position exudes influential ethos.

Nice story.
What's the point?

A story is not a speech.

A story is a story.

I've heard plenty of speakers tell a story, many times great stories at that, and conclude at the story's end, believing, mistakenly, they had delivered a speech.

A speech requires a message.

The delivery of the message through the speech is how we reinforce or change audience thoughts or behaviours.

Now that I have **your** attention

Speeches that contain stories, anecdotes, metaphors, and analogies have a greater persuasive effect on audiences because of their innate ability to connect and engage audiences. The stories themselves however, are merely a delivery mechanism for the message.

A speech's message is illustrated within the poignant points of the selected story. Without a message you are merely storytelling.

Stories have an uncanny ability to toy with audience emotions. Plenty of presenters draw on personal experiences of illnesses, injuries, adversity, or survival. Often the presentations are rich with struggle, pain, loss and tragedy, and climax with demonstrations of resilience, triumph, or emotional resolution.

Every story has the power to move an audience to tears, and everyone has a powerful story. But a great speaker wants more than tears. They aspire to achieve action from those tears.

To initiate action there must be a point to the story; the message.

The emotionally charged story typically holds the spotlight of the presentation. A speaker with an illness recovery account can powerfully couple their story with a call to donate to vaccination

Nice story. What's the point?

research, or persuade people to invest in income insurance, or inspire people to live each day as though it were gold.

Stories are wonderful and amazingly powerful in their place but alone they do not qualify as speeches.

The skill is balancing the right story against the purpose of your presentation and crafting the underlying message around and through it. It isn't complicated turning a story into a speech with a message.

Have a look at the following snippet taken from one of my own speeches on the next page. This particular speech is on quite a controversial topic.

You'll notice the high story-to-message ratio, as well as the power simplicity can generate. Stories don't have to be born from high octane drama to create the equivalent emotional response in your audience.

The key ingredient is connection;

- » connection between the message and the story,
- » and connection between the story and the audience.

Now that I have your attention

Don't overlook any part of your own experience as a potential story or how it might relate to your audience. The purpose, in this instance, was to generate debate, not to persuade an audience to a particular viewpoint.

The part in *italics* is the story, the part in **bold** makes it a speech.

It was a cool spring morning, 25 years ago. I was driving from our small farm to the local service station to buy some milk. I had a lot on my mind.

From the corner of my eye I spotted, what appeared to be, two birds fighting on the side of the road. I drove on thinking it didn't look like a fair fight.

I hit the brakes, performed the most dramatic U-turn, and headed back to the battle ground.

I screeched to a halt. As I jumped out of my car, the bigger bird, a large black crow, took three or four hops away. The smaller bird, a chicken, remained motionless. I assumed that chicken had somehow fallen from one of the many trucks that passed our house nightly en route to the local abattoir.

This poor disheveled mess of a bird looked up at me. Now, I'm not claiming to be an expert on avian facial expressions, but her eyes didn't show fear. What I saw was resignation. The chook had had its day, and it knew it.

Nice story. What's the point?

I knelt beside her and started stroking her head. The crow looked on.

"You must be the luckiest chicken in the world. You somehow managed to escape your fate as someone's Sunday dinner, only to be attacked by him, and now I come along. I'm going to take you home so you can live out your days scratching around my yard with my three fat laying hens. I'm going to call you 'Lucky '."

It was at this point that I more closely examined her blood stained back. Her injuries were so severe that there was no chance of her survival. I sat silent, still stroking her head. I knew what I had to do. I placed my hands around her neck and with a crack, I ended her suffering.

I picked her up, took her to the car and placed her in a plastic bag. I would take her home and bury her.

As I sat behind the steering wheel I began to cry. I am not usually a crier, but today was a particularly emotional day. Later that morning we would bury my father, his body having been pecked away by the black crow of cancer.

Lucky had made me realise my selfishness.

I had been saying, "Please let me have one more year with Dad, one more month, one more day".

Over the last months of his life, we had watched this sweet, wonderful and gentle man be robbed of his health, his faculties, and his dignity, often in a drug-induced stupor.

Now that I have **your** attention

> **I had looked into his fading eyes which conveyed resignation time and time again, asking him to stay a bit longer.**
>
> **Why couldn't this dear man have been released from his misery?**
>
> **Few of you will argue that what I did for Lucky, the chicken, wasn't merciful. Yet if my father's doctor had ended his suffering a few weeks earlier, he could have found himself behind bars, facing very different public opinion. Is that right?**

The purpose of the speech was to open a conversation about euthanasia. The story about Lucky intentionally and clearly dominated the speech. It was specially selected to pull contrasting relatable situations into a single confrontational argument to achieve the outcome.

If I had just told the story of two birds fighting, resulting in the grim fate of one, it would just have been a poignant but potential unremarkable event in the minds of the audience unlikely to generate later reflection by anyone other than "Corvid" or poultry lovers. If I had just asked the audience to share their thoughts on euthanasia I'd have probably been pecked upon like Lucky!

Go be spectacular

You are unique. I am unique.

Each and every person in this vast world is unique. The chances of any one of us coming into existence just the way we are, is almost unimaginable. Your parents had to meet, and that one swimmer had to meet that particular egg. The same with their parents and so on, all the way back to the start of our species.

The Buddhists describe it like this:

> Imagine you are on a boat in the middle of the ocean, and in all the oceans of the world, there is only one turtle. You throw a life ring into the water, and, as it is about to land, the turtle surfaces and the ring slips around its neck. That you are here, as you are, has the same probability.

With that in mind, we should make the most of this rare opportunity. If we have something

Now that I have **your** attention

to say that can make this world a better place, improve lives, bring hope or joy, I believe we have an obligation to say it as best we can.

The tips in this book are here to help you stand out like the tulip in a field of green grass.

Don't be afraid to be spectacular. Tell stories, make people laugh, teach and inspire.

If this book helps one person to do these things, my job is done.

If this book helps one person, let it be you.

www.ingramcontent.com/pod-product-compliance
Lightning Source LLC
Chambersburg PA
CBHW050316010526
44107CB00055B/2271